Birthing Butterflies

poems by

Claudia May

Finishing Line Press
Georgetown, Kentucky

Birthing Butterflies

Dedicated to Anarcha, Betsey, Lucy and the other Black enslaved women, their ancestors, and legacy bearers.

In the name of human dignity and vulnerability, these women of courage continue to fight, live, love, and pursue humane liberation.

This work is also dedicated to my grandmother and mother—I am because you birthed my becoming.

And I honor my dear deceased sister-friend and phenomenal mother, Lisa Gervers—you are missed but not forgotten.

Copyright © 2024 by Claudia May
ISBN 979-8-88838-794-8 First Edition
All rights reserved under International and Pan-American Copyright Conventions. No part of this book may be reproduced in any manner whatsoever without written permission from the publisher, except in the case of brief quotations embodied in critical articles and reviews.

Publisher: Leah Huete de Maines
Editor: Christen Kincaid
Cover Art: Unsplash, created by Susan Wikinson
Interior Artwork: istockphoto.com
Author Photo: Anna Min
Cover Design: Elizabeth Maines McCleavy

Order online: www.finishinglinepress.com
 also available on amazon.com

Author inquiries and mail orders:
Finishing Line Press
PO Box 1626
Georgetown, Kentucky 40324
USA

Contents

Preface ix
Epigraph x
Adult Butterflies 1
Nanny Mama Parables—Love 2
De Rivah 3
Oh To Be A Black Cottonwood Tree In Bloom
—An Ode to Janie Mae Crawford 4
When Black Love Is A Black Cottonwood Tree 6
Un-Enslaved Love 7
Song of Songs Spirit Blues Love 8
Love As De Sun 9
Senses 10
Harvest Baby 11
Home 13
The Eggs 14
Nanny Mama Parables—Birthin' 15
Love Live 16
Slavery Cain't Enslave De Word—NO! 17
Speak Life Befo' Baby Born 18
Birth Prayah 19
When Pregnancy Skin Sing De Blues 20
Womb 21
When Touch Breathes 22
Work Labor Premature Birth Blues 24
Baby Dead Rap Blues 25
When Dem Love Me Tradition 26
Anarcha Had a Baby,
(An ode to the spiritual, "Mary Had a Baby") 27
Sleep Lullaby 28
Caterpillars 29
Nanny Mama Parables—Freedom 30
Nevah Alone 31
Givin' Birth 33
Here 35
Postnatal Depression Blues 36
Bedtime Morn' 37
Nanny Teach 38
Breathtaking Sweetness 39

Love Lullaby	40
Chrysalis	41
Nanny Mama Parables—Fear	42
Befo' De Surgery: He Tell Doctor Man	43
Lament	44
During De Surgery: What's Happenin' To Me?	46
Slice: For Anarcha	47
Blood Alive When Dead	50
Contraction Abuse Blues	51
Cotton Legacy	52
Aftah De Surgery: What Happened To Me?	54
Trauma Shadows	55
"Den Dis Baby Be Sleep"	56
Butterflies Breaking Through Chrysalises	57
Nanny Mama Parables—Survival	58
Blood Mothahs	59
Stillborn Wisdom Blues	61
The Dawn Of A Sky	62
When Loss Astonishes	63
When A Black Enslaved Nature Woman Philosophizes	64
Watched	65
Butterfly Movements	66
Nanny Mama Parables—Wisdom	67
Secrets	68
Nanny Mama Medicine	69
De Womb Tree	71
Return	72
Breathin' Don' Regret Breathin'	73
Pass It Forward	74
Questions From a Son to a Mother	75
Yesterday Becoming	76
Grief Songs	77
Liberation	78
My Tongue	80
Air Love	81
Ancestors	82
Way Up Yonder	83
Full Circle Butterfly Unbroken By Life	85
Nanny Mama Parables—Birth Cycle	86
A Poetic Memorial for Black Mothers—Past, Present, and the Future	89
Acknowledgments	95
Notes	96

Preface

Birthing Butterflies is inspired by nineteenth-century Black enslaved mothers and their experiences of childbirth, motherhood, and community. These poems unearth the loving relationships and support systems Black women cultivated while navigating brutal systemic methods of control. These poems are meant to be read and pondered on their own terms. I respect the reader's imagination and ability to conjure meanings and unravel interpretations to enliven each poetic narrative.

For those who identify with the histories and poetic spoken words featured in this work, may these truth-tellings and cultural practices draw you deeper into your heritage memories. May you feel the fullness of your beautiful and complex humanity alongside your ancestors. May their innovations and courage fill you with pride and foster a sense of belonging. May their experiences shed light on your present day challenges, bring insight into how to confront injustices, and stimulate ways of being that lead to collective liberation.

For those unfamiliar with Black English and the spellings of nineteenth-century Black linguistic expressions, I encourage you to read these poems aloud. Allow the sounds of each word to sing to you. The oral tradition honors the stories, rhythmic speech patterns and tonalities articulated by Black enslaved communities. Still, I realize that some may find the concluding essay entitled, "A Poetic Memorial for Black Mothers—Past, Present, and the Future," to be a helpful entry point when first reading this collection. The essay provides context surrounding the historical events underscoring these poems.

Birthing Butterflies acknowledges the existence of medical racism and exposes its trauma symptoms. And yet, in the midst of a violent and inhumane socio-economic system, the Black individuals lining these pages birth life into love. They cherish one another. They suckle on their belovedness. Enslavement neither defines their character nor consumes their being. So, in the name of healing, this is where our poetic affirmation of their vital humanity begins—in the womb of gentleness and creative, liberating love.

Survival cannot survive without surviving.
Survival cannot survive without living.

The words we share hold our stories
For those who dare to listen and live and fly . . .

Adult Butterflies

ARCHIPPUS.—*Dánais archippus.*

A butterfly don' love jus' anybody.

Nanny Mama Parables—Love

I
Love run
When love flow.

II
Lovin' yo' baby,
Lovin' yo'se'f,
De same thing.

III
Don' love nobody
Ef you don' love yo'se'f.

IV
Love you mean love us.
Love us mean love you.

V
Sometimes de love ov someone
Teach us how love live.
Sometimes love cain't wait to love
When de harvest good an' done.

VI
Love lak a creek.
It cain't reflect what it cain't see an' feel.

VII
Love cain't be clear ov agony
If metal rods calve shackles.

De Rivah

Her body lak a rivah
Dat don' travel by herse'f.
Wherevah she go
Ancestor ring roun' her.
Her spirit spiral
As an amblin' moonflowah.
She don' bleed dry.

Her body lak a rivah
Surrounded by hibiscus
Lovin' each othah alive.
De sassafras an' sweet gum tree
Glory in demse'f
When dem leaf
Turn beetroot
Okra
Fig pulp
An' lemon melon rind.

Seasons unwrap seasons.
De earth still lives.
De rivah an' red maple tree
Don' change each othah
Into somethin' we nevah believe.

Oh To Be A Black Cottonwood Tree In Bloom
—An Ode to Janie Mae Crawford

The sixteen-year-old
Stretches upwards
As branches massage the sky.
Curiosity
Ebbs and flows in her mind
Like wrinkles
Ribbing the surface of a stream.
Sweat lines her limbs.
Cotton garlands shrubs.
Moonlight unveils dust.
Dreams rest in her mind
As day unfurls,
Her view clear.

She wears sixteen
Like a Black cottonwood tree
Garnished with new clothes of spring.
Green shoots
Poke out their heads
Through branches
Hewed with the ages.
They emerge
As unfurled moth wings
Layered into pear-shaped molds.

Twilight delivers dawn.
Winds comb wool-like blossoms.
Each fleecy strand
Curves with the murmur of the breeze,
Releasing other threads to break free
From clusters of jade pods.
Unable to contain their elation,
They tumble into the rumble of rain.

Flowering with spring tide,
The woman-girl reclines
Against a sapling.
Her nutmeg copper skin
Blends with her toffee tinted torso.
Like caramelized buds
Sunned in the clotted heat of June,
Her breasts nourish promises
Yet to be relished.

The humid glaze of noon
Lingers in her skin.
Sweat abandons her pores.
Her body trembles
Under the low-lying arch
Of the one whose body
Waters her parched belly.

Her forearms
Sleeved with goosebumps
Accompany wonder.
Flies stagger as they stammer.
Their hums cascade
Into wordless sonnets.
Cobwebs glistening with dew
Shudder.

Hummingbird mint percolates the air.

The girl-woman inhales chocolate daisies
Teeming with virgin florets,
Aroused by the prospect
Of more sprays to come.

Her pulse simmers.
Coves of pleasure
Loosen her tears.
Untainted by remorse,
Her flesh,
Honeyed with delight,
Shivers.

Her imagination
Flushes her daydreams.
She listens to cotton
Pearled with ebony seeds
Breaking the seals of their shells.
They harmonize
Unforgotten sacraments
Of unsilenced souls
Resounding
With the echoes of trees
Living in her body.

When Black Love Is A Black Cottonwood Tree

Your kisses
Light as purple lovegrass
Shawl my shoulders

Like balmy molasses
Your lips
Lacquered
Full of me
Thick with us
Nibble
L e i s u r e l y
Down
My skin

Our love
Unhindered
Nests
Among cornflowers
And like pollen
Pauses in unsung places

When I plant my hands in yours
Our twined fingers
Turn into a spring garden
Lavender lilacs call home

When we whisper to each other
Cottonwood plumes fall
Like freshly unplaited afro braids
Dressed in fullness

Our limp limbs languish
The gales gasp
As glassy paw paw pips
Scatter across an open earth

Un-Enslaved Love

        I

Her skin
Pollinates
The strange fruit of pleasure
Basking in her body.

Her gaze savors the man
Lying next to her.
She smells his torso.
Honey salt and musk
Soak in her pores.

When they roll together,
Unruly wild grass
Sways with them.
Their bodies churn
Into one another,
Folding rhythms
Of their own making
Until exhaustion
Slackens their dance
And they arise as loose vines
Lavished with wisteria and magnolia.

Dusk
Mushrooms in their bones.
Their tide
Mellows their bodies.
She laughs.
He giggles.

They rest in each other's shade.

        II

We garden our stories together
Nurse our hopes and hold hands
We argue
We listen to one another
Even when we disagree
We rub each other's weary hands at the end of an unkind day
We see ourselves in each other's eyes
For our people, we cook ash cakes, collards, and any meat or fish we catch
We praise one another
We share our fears and anger and worries
We admit our mistakes and forgive one another
We sun ourselves in delight
We cherish our community and family
We free

Song of Songs Spirit Blues Love

You my,
summah fierce undah a dry sky befo' sunset slink across land an' sink down down
down.
You my, dip dip dippin' into my hot slick bush burstin' wid sticky sweet honeysuckle
smellin' ov us.
You my, my, my I cain't see cuz laughter weep in my eyes an' spill all ovah
my blues blue blue heart.
You my, my my my please keep on lettin' yo' skin shine up my flesh
lak a mellow buttercream tangerine moon.
You my, rain-soak ground moist wid petals,
wet from de steam ov stewin' high mornin'
rise rise rise.
You my, back rubbin' against de grass dat feel lak its green blade soakin' in syrup while
we sing sing sing
wid de birds kind-ov-love.

What's dat you say?

You my,
summah fierce undah a dry sky befo' sunset slink across land an' sink down down
down.
You my, dip dip dippin' into my hot slick bush burstin' wid sticky sweet honeysuckle
smellin' ov us.
You my, my, my I cain't see cuz laughter weep in my eyes an' spill all ovah
my blues blue blue heart.
You my, oh my my my please keep on lettin' yo' skin shine up my flesh
lak a mellow buttercream tangerine moon.
You my, rain-soak ground moist wid petals,
wet from de steam ov stewin' high mornin'
rise rise rise.
You my, back rubbin' against de grass dat feel lak its green blade soakin' in syrup while
we sing sing sing
wid de birds kind-ov-love.

You ready now?

Love As De Sun

Our love cain't be caught,
Same as de sun.
It free.
It shine.
It free.
It shine.

Senses

Your cocoa flesh
Fragile as first frost
Coats faint maroon veins
My fingers skim your forehead
As heat bumps rise

When I see you
I imagine woodlands
Clutching birch roots
Supple as spring leaves
Uneven as broken bark

When I smell you
I inhale
New rain
Spiked with aromas
Of damp soil and Indian blanket flowers

When I hear you
I listen to indigo gusts
Chant,
We the sunrise
That never stops opening

Harvest Baby

We haul crop
Pack it
Ready it up fo' sale

Don' wa'n't you in my belly
When I pick cotton
An' my fingah bleed
Blistah wince
An' summah slicken my skin

Don' wa'n't carry you
In my belly
When ovahripe August sun
Toast my back

So we wait
Wait
Till evenin' sleep early

We watch
De cold blue moon
We watch
Shasta daisy stars beam
We watch
De burnt orange Octobah sun
Undress dusk
We watch
Decembah pluck tree branch clean
Wintah hatch
As ef dead bird
Covah in smash egg shell

Den
Den
Ol' Nanny Mama
Search bush
Pick livin' leaves
Boil tea
Tell me drink it

When crop harvest
I know time come
Fo' desiah to climb in
My body

Dat's when breeze
Smell lak leaf
Dead in mournin'
Dat's when Laurenzi an' me
Create our honey cherry berry
Sweet baby unborn chile
As dazzlin' as de yellow lips
Ov a violet iris
Befo' sunup smile

Home[1]

Lovely darlin' Delia,
Honey baby sweet girl,
You mus' have been no mo' dan six,
Maybe seven months in my belly
When you journey
In my dream story.

Befo' you bawn,
Yo' mouth full ov gums.
I see you smile
When I tek you in my arms.
Yo' chubby legs dance wid de air
As I sing,

"Come, Mammy, come.
Come, Mammy, come.
Lil' girl sittin' in de briar bush
Waitin' for de Mammy to come."

You so bendy,
Sometime you wriggle yo' foot
Lak you some rag doll.
Ahhh,
When you suck yo' thumb,
You look at me
Lak I yo' sky.
You watch my lips move
As ef you lookin' at cloud
Crawlin' lak slug.
You babble baby noise
Only you understan'.
Sweat peppah yo' nose-bridge.
Yo' eyes leap wid de lullaby beat.

When yo' fingahs pat my chin,
I sing:

"No more waitin' for Mammy to come."

Lovely darlin' Delia,
Mama here,
Mama home.

[1] McGill, Alice, editor. *In the Hollow of Your Hand: Slave Lullabies.* Houghton Mifflin, 2000. Inspired by the lullaby, "Lil' Girl Sittin' in de Briar Bush," created by one or more Black innovators enslaved during the antebellum era.

The Eggs

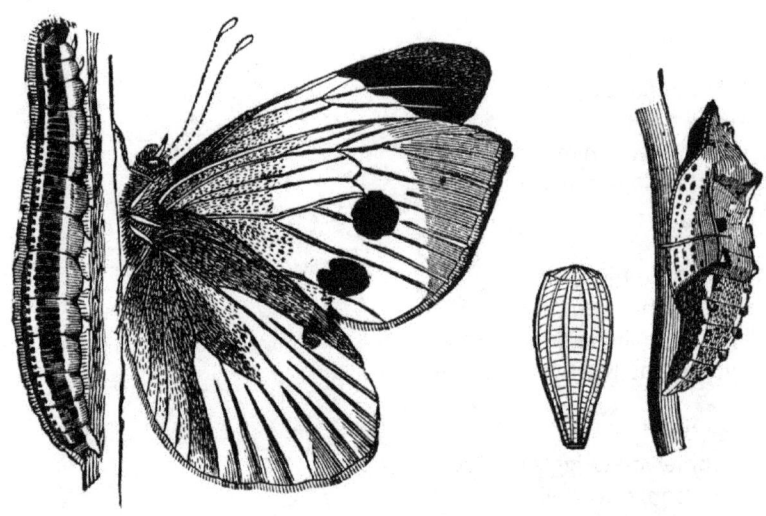

A butterfly cain't create new life widout anotha butterfly. A butterfly cain't give birth to itse'f.

Nanny Mama Parables—Birthin'

I
Plant yo' baby aftah-birth
Undah a tree.
Den dem root will hol' hands
Wid tree root in Affica.
An' covah yo' aftah-birth wid onion and peppah
So dog cain't dig it up.

II
Give yo' baby
De first ov yo' breas' milk,
Befo' Mastah Man chillun.

III
Ef baby bite you
When it suck yo' breas'
An' you say it hurt,
Don' mean you don' love yo' chile.

IV
Ef yo' breas' milk squeeze starvin,'
Let anotha sistah feed yo' chile.
Remembah,
She don' have to be kin.

V
New Mama,
We love you an' de baby dat's in you.

VI
Slavery nevah did
Or nevah will have
De first or last word
On birthin' love.

VII
When you tired
You tired.

Love Live

Today,
I step out ov my baby skin,
Belly full wid first chile.

Mama pass.
Mama gone.
She drift on de othah side.

Papa sold.
Papa gone.
He trap in places dat don' know me.

Mama an' Papa
Roost in me.
Dem love go on fruitin'
In me.

Slavery Cain't Enslave De Word—NO!

                        I say **NO!**

Ovahseeah ordah someone
Dig hole deepah dan a big ole burnt dutch pot
Den him elbow my belly puff-up wid chile
Inna dirt womb
An' whip me up an' down my Black bare back

Him nevah slash my belly
Cuz he wanna protect my chile
So he can mek mo' money fo' Mastah
On auction day

                        I wail **NO!**

Ovahseeah tell someone
Tie me to a tree
So him can slit me
Wid his cowhide whip

When it claw at my heavy breas'
My blood an' milk
Rush de same way as watahfall
De color ov a newborn pink rose

                        I shout

                        NO!

                        NO!

                        NO!

My mind mumble
As ef I'm talkin' undah watah
Irons crack in me
As ef I'm a cut down willow tree
Wid a noose aroun' its roots
But my heart still drum

When I walk wid ancestors
My feet break into
Mastah's tough-sof' shoes
An' I keep runnin' from slavery
Inside my voice

Speak Life Befo' Baby Born

You de wind
Racin' across acre
Wid no end in sight

You de sun
Huggin' sky
Wid no end in sight

You firefly bright
Shinin' freckles ov light
Wid no end in sight

You de Seven Pointers
Lacein' night
Wid no end in sight

When noon boil soil to dust
Causin' shoots to hang dem head down low
Our love yo' backbone

When storm bully land
Throwin' thunder an' tramplin' tree
Our love yo' shelter

When heat knot air
Chokin' de flurry till it cain't hush
Our love yo' breath
Our love yo' harbor

Birth Prayah

God,
Don' let me give birth
When sun hot.

Jesus,
Don' let me give birth
When sun burn.

Spirit,
Don' let me give birth
When sun white.

When Pregnancy Skin Sing De Blues

My skin
Look sad.
Her glow done gone.

My skin
Look lak dead ash
When fire wood melt.

My skin
Coarse
Lak crack tree bark.

My skin
Bow lak branch
Mournin' fo' summah leaves
To shine.

Womb

You nest in my womb,
A low hangin' moon.
Yo' glisten guide my course.

Befo' my belly big
You as airy as new baby hair.

You lak
Black-Eyed Susans
Glowin'
Widin me.

No torch can blind
You.
No coop can fence
You.
No sky can swamp
You.
No law can vanish
You.
No Mastah Man can wrestle
You
Away from de skyline
We
Haven't created
Fo' ourse'f
Yet.

Only one drinkin' gourd
Kindle sky.
Only one ov you
Walk currents
Wid our foremothahs
On paths dat bend
Aroun' cornah
We cain't see

Yet.

When Touch Breathes

My baby stirs
In my womb
As night swaddles dusk
I place my hand
On my belly
And allow my fingers
Swollen by time
To brush my skin
In circles
It feels like velvet
Dusted with sand

My baby feels like a girl
I imagine putting my finger
On the hollow ridge
Between her nose and lips
A half curled petal
Her breath
Tender as dandelion cotton

You my baby girl will teach me
How to cherish the seasons
As I learn to treasure you

And so

I inhale jasmine
As rain freckles the sky
I lift my face towards its embrace

Summer lulls me
Into its sultry lavender glory
Wild red berries pearl
Along shrubs
The haze of blue skies
Mists my gaze

I marinate in autumn
Musk swells the gusts
Cold metal gales
Yank life off branches
Bronze leaf embers
Quilt rural pathways

I soak in winter
Smell the spice of wood fires
Watch charcoal storms
Create new tracks
Across crossroads

And I
Ripe with you
Nesting in my belly
Will stroke the soft-spoken earth
Anew

Work Labor Premature Birth Blues

When my belly big
I lift up basket loaded wid soggy linen
I worry dis bulk too heavy
Fo' my unborn chile
To survive livin'

When my belly big
I kneel an' scrub sheets
Till my hands strip raw
I worry I'm bendin' too much
Fo' my unborn chile
To last out livin'

When my belly big
I pick crop
As heat rise up my body
Lak kettle steam
My shin trap sharp glass pain
Lak a purse shut tight
I worry de bakin' wetha too much
Fo' my unborn chile
To pull thro' livin'

When my belly big
My baby boy born small
Him born little
Him born fightin'
Him born dead.

Baby Dead Rap Blues

Baby Dead
Baby Gone
Gone
Baby Pass
Baby Stiff
Stiff
Baby Hard
Baby Still
Still
Baby Leave
Baby Cold
Cold
Baby Gray
Baby Pale
Pale
Baby Gone
Baby Dead
Dead

When Dem Love Me Tradition

Befo' my chile call me Mama,
My own Mama an' Papa
Call me precious.
Dey wa'n't me befo' I wa'n't myse'f.
Dey love me befo'
I know love.

My people
Hug me.
Dem kiss me.
Dem see de sun
In me.

My people
Listen to de rain
In me.
Dem relieve hurricane
In me.
Dem map Ellen Yards
In me.
Dem wish gaze
In me.
Dem watch sunup
In me.
Dem plant fragrant tea olive
In me.
Dem watah roots
In me.
Dem hear de bird choir
In me.
Dem prize de meadow
In me.

Anarcha Had a Baby, (An ode to the spiritual, "Mary Had a Baby")

Anarcha had a baby,
Yes, Lawd.
Anarcha had a baby,
Yes, my Lawd.
Huuuuuummbbbbbb.
Huuuuuummbbbbbb.

Anarcha had a baby,
Yes, Lawd.
Anarcha had a baby,
Yes, my Lawd.
Huuuuuummbbbbbb.
Huuuuuummbbbbbb.
She sure did.
She sure did.

Anarcha had a baby,
Yes, Lawd.
Clap, clap, clapclap, clap
Clapclapclapclapclapclap
Yes,
Yes,
Yes, my Lawd.
Yes, my Lawd.

Anarcha had a baby,
Yes, Lawd.
Anarcha had a baby,
Stomp yo' feet.
Stomp stompstomp stomp stomp stomp,
Stompstompstompstompstomp,
Clapclapstompstompclapclapclapclapstomp.
Glory. Hah!
Glory. Hah!
Glory. Hah!

Yesssssss,
Yesssssss,
Anarcha had a baby,
Yes, Lawd.
Huuuuuummbbbbbb.
Huuuuuummbbbbbb.
Yes, my Lawd
Yes, my Lawd.
Yes, my Lawd.
Hah!

Sleep Lullaby[2]

"Save all your kisses, sleep baby,"
Don' let no one kiss someone fo' you.
"Save all your kisses, sleep baby,"
Don' let no one snatch your kisses.
"Save all your kisses, sleep baby,"
Let sleep kiss you goodnight.

Sshhhh sleep
Sshhhh

"Save all your hugs, sleep baby,"
Don' let no one hug you fo' demse'f.
"Save all your hugs, sleep baby,"
Don' let no one hug you fo' sale.
"Save all your hugs, sleep baby,"
Let sleep hug you goodnight.

Sshhh sleep
Sshhh

Mama here
Mama here

See?

---

[2] McGill, Alice, editor. *In the Hollow of Your Hand: Slave Lullabies.* Houghton Mifflin, 2000. Inspired by the lullaby, "Every Little Bit," created by one or more Black innovators enslaved during the antebellum era.

Caterpillars

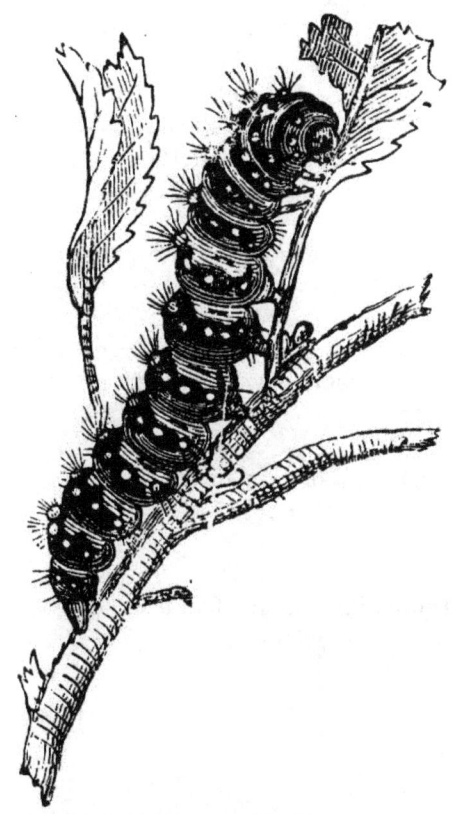

CATERPILLAR OF PEACOCK-
BUTTERFLY.

A catahpillah don' ask permission to eat when it need growin.'

Nanny Mama Parables—Freedom

I
We cain't escape freedom
Cuz freedom live in us.

II
Freedom don' throw me away
Cuz I don' treat myse'f lak scrap.

III
My mind cain't be enslaved
Cuz my mind free.

IV
Freedom move in her own time.

V
Freedom say don' seek anythin' or anyone
Dat don' wa'n't you free.

VI
Freedom my house.
My house freedom.

VII
Let freedom put her feet up on de porch
Ov yo' mind, body, spirit.

Nevah Alone

Befo' Mama Ruth birth babies
Befo' she share her workin' cure
Her hand slick as buttermilk
Rub me down
Wid chamomile an' soap
My spirit roam her voice
Vivid as marigold

When birthin' my chile
I suck air thro' tight teeth
Mama Nanny sing
As she give me watah

s t e a d i l y

s t e a d i l y

When my head fire-up fevah
Lak summah stew in flame
Mama Nanny lay damp cloth ovah my eyes

t e n d e r l y

t e n d e r l y

Mama Nanny wander free
She burn sage in de room
To drive away grave-ghost
Dat don' protect me—
Wisdom smoke
Heal my soul

f r e e l y

f r e e l y

She hear me complain
I scrunch up lak an ol' woman
My body a sack ov stones
But she crouch wid me

p a t i e n t l y

p a t i e n t l y

When my body sink to de floor
She put my arm aroun' her shouldah
An' walk me across de room
When my hips won't lie down
She stroke my neck
Fingahs lak feathas
Whisperin' to me

g e n t l y

g e n t l y

When cramp jab me
Mama Ruth tell me push
I squeeze her hand
While she cradle my yellin'

Mama Nanny words
Smooth as peach-corn sky
An' when she pat my back
Her palm feel July warm

She look in my eyes
She call my name

s o f t l y

s o f t l y

When my baby shout at de world
She snuggle her
Wrap her wid wisdom-love
Wash her down
Lak she wash me

D e l i c a t e l y

B e a u t i f u l l y

Givin' Birth

My fingahs grab air
Prayin' to tek me out ov my body
My lips split as ef smash cracklin'
I yell
Lawd
HELP ME

I push

Bruise pinch every inch
Ov my tree thigh
Hard
Every scrap ov me
Throw up fire
My back feel
As ef hot iron glue my skin
My nails scratch de wind
I howl
I cain't
I jus'
Cain't

I push

My womb feel lak grown men
Kickin' me wid dem fist
Forest burn thro' my hips
Fry my bones

I push

My hands collapse
Body crumble
Lak wet clothes
Drop from washin' line

My baby girl
Burst into de world
Grabbin' Big Dippah hand

Belief kiss her lung
Her body
Plump wid quiet breath
Come alive

She cry

It was den
I learn
How to breathe
Fo' de first time

                                      Again

Here

When my baby
Push her way
Out ov my body
Mess an' blood
An' white powder-liquid
Lak de lace peel
Ov cooled hot milk
Covah her

I sweep tiredness away
An' holler
She HERE
She *Here*
She H e r e

My baby

She H E R E...

Postnatal Depression Blues

I feel blue
My body won't
Eat collards or cornmeal
Molasses or chicken
Cain't sniff food smell
It don' wa'n't nothin' no mo'
It jus' let my belly grumble

I feel blue
My body won't
Sing "Go Down Moses"
An' let my moan
Yawn from gut to lung
So my song words
Bob an' dip wid de wind
Hummin' real sof'

I feel blue
My body won't
Dance de giouba wid me
Won't shuffle feet
Bend knee
Lift leg an' kick
Twist an' whoop
Clap an' ring shout

I feel blue
My body won't
Laugh at chicken play tag
As de hen an' cock rock-walk from side-to-side
Racin' across yard an' coop
Stumblin' lak dem drunk
As ef pants wrap aroun' dem ankle
Tight tight
An' dem cain't stand
Straight straight

Lawd God Almighty, I feel so so blue

My womb empty
My baby touch me
But I cain't feel myse'f

Oh Lawd I don' know why
I feel so blue

    So so so blue

Bedtime Morn'

You sleep
While mulberry skies
Hum rhyme
To you.

I settle yo' head against my neck.
You fill my smell
As ef pasture
Weave wid flowerin' dogwood.

I play
Wid de kink in yo' hair
When it damp.
It feel lak windflower petal
Rinse wid summah shower.

When day bristle
You bawl.

You warm.
You alive.
You warm.
You alive.

Nanny Teach

One-by-one,
Nanny teach us
How we help baby
Suck milk from our breas.'

One-by-one,
Nanny teach us
How to wrap cloth
Aroun' waist an' chest
To carry chile
On our back.

One-by-one,
Nanny teach us
What to do
When milk
Stop livin'
Or baby
Bite breas.'

One-by-one,
Nanny listen
When we sore.
She show us
What to do
When we afraid,
When we cain't tek care
Ov baby
Ourse'f.

Nanny feel lak gust
Coolin' August glare.

Nanny Love.
Nanny Affica.
Nanny Vegetable Garden.
Nanny Risin' Roses an' Chinaberry Trees.
Nanny Backwoods.
Nanny Home.

Breathtaking Sweetness

Your dimples feel like dough
Moistened with molasses,
Pudgy with sticky sweetness.
The folds of your arms and legs
Resemble cotton pillows
Browned like russet chestnuts.
I trace my fingers along your toes,
Each nail clear as rain.
Furrows crinkle down your soles.

I cup your feet,
Soft as feather grass,
While pride ferries my joy
To you.

As your eyes dwell on my face,
What do you see?

Do you see yourself in me?

Do you see how my eyes mirror glints of a spring dawn?

Do you see how my oiled Black plaits
Sculpt my face like a magnolia haloed by August mist?

Do you see how hints of auburn
Tint my pecan skin?

Do you see how my love
Tosses daffodils into a winter night?

Do you know
We created the skin of your seasons
Only you will wear?

Love Lullaby[3]

My honey baby girl
Mama gonna give you
"Every little bit added to what you got
Hmmm . . ."

I bury my nose in yo' neck roll
An' call out

Mama gonna give you
"Every little bit added to what you got
Hmmm . . ."

You pat my cheeks
An' I speak music
De rise an' fall
Is a love song
I sing to you

"Every little bit added to what you got
Will make you have a little bit more. . ."

You born wid no hair
My kiss de oil
Dat mek each bushy curl grow

You honey sugar baby girl
Can nevah have enough
"little bit more" love

---

[3] McGill, Alice, editor. *In the Hollow of Your Hand: Slave Lullabies.* Houghton Mifflin, 2000. Inspired by the lullaby, "Every Little Bit," created by one or more Black innovators enslaved during the antebellum era.

Chrysalis

A chrysalis cain't hang by itse'f; it need somethin' to hang onto.

Nanny Mama Parables—Fear

I
Don' follow fear
Where hope dead.

II
Fear don' love you.

III
Don' let fear be yo' name.

IV
Don' give fear yo' breas' milk.

V
Lak air, fear everywhere.
But don' mek fear yo' breath.

VI
Fear hate God
Cuz God ain't afraid ov fear.

VII
Fear can die
Ef you let it.

Befo' De Surgery: He Tell Doctor Man

Him say
Operate
I say
Don' wa'n't nobody dig into me

He tell Doctor Man
Operate
My fear run into my head
She feel safe in me
Cuz I hear her
See her
Understan' her
Believe her

He tell Doctor Man
He *need* me to breed
My spirit say
No

He tell Doctor Man
My babies mek money
My body say
My life my life

He tell Doctor Man
He *need* me to breed
My soul say
I bring life into de world fo' myse'f

He tell Doctor Man
Do what I say because I Mastah I AM
When Mastah speak
His word
Try tug breath from my lungs
But de wind still blow

                Blow

                                      Blow

Lament

Muscles scowl
Vaginal walls split
Wounds heave
My bladder blubbers
My baby preaches
I berate the world

Battered by labor
My bowel
Forces my waste to ebb
With its impulses
Stench fouls my clothes
Ulcers corrode my reddened thighs
Urine laces raw buttocks
Yet I can still smell
My newborn's carnation scent
Inside me

The experiments begin
When I am 17-years-old

Doctor Man, Mastah Man, Missus
Call me slave
I call myse'f Woman
They call me slave
I call myse'f Mama
They call me slave
I call myse'f Many
They call me slave
I call myse'f Me

In five years
The surgeon cuts into me
Thirty times
Plows into my vagina
Thirty times
Clubs my nerves
Thirty times

After he invades my body
After his handprints litter my bladder
He sews up my shredded vagina scars
Stashes his fingerprints into the stitches
For safekeeping

Still

Just as air
Refuses to be caged
Just as shadows
Evade being pinned down
Time cannot forget itself

My body stores my stories
Unraveling with no end

The thunder
Scoops up my tears
Rocks them in its arms
And lets sorrow
Sob

Lament suckles my memories
My eyes see me
Beyond the glare of those
Who see through me

Still

I nuzzle the quilts of fat
Circling the neck
Of my baby honey girl
As an act of prayer
I stroke her eyebrows
Each touch marvels
At the gift of her life

Elders knead bee balm into my scalp till it glistens
Then braid my hair
My man
Blessed with blueberry skin
Caresses my back
Bathes my legs and feet
In warm water
Swimming with goldenrod and orange peel

As the aroma of sweet peas
Mounts the breeze
My people
Chant the voices of ancestors

I am alive to my name

Anarcha

During De Surgery: What's Happenin' To Me?

What's happenin' to me? What'S HAPPENIN' to me? WHAT's hapP ENIN' to ME? What's HAPP-E-NIN' TO ME? **S'TAHW HAPPENIN' TO EM**? What's *happenin'* to me? What's happenin' to me? What's happenin' to ME? WHAT is happenin' to m-e? What's HappeNiN' to me? What's HAPPENIN' to me? What'*s happenin'* to me? What's happenin' to me¿ What's happenin' to me? What's happenin' to me? What's happenin' to me? What's happenin' to me? What's happenin' to me? What's happenin' to me? **What's   happenin'   to   em!** What'S HAPPENIN' to me? WHAT's hapP ENIN' to ME? What'S HAPP-E-NIN' TO ME? WHAT'S HAPPENIN' TO ME? What's happenin' to me? What's happenin' to me? What's happenin' to ME? WHAT's happenin' to m-e? What's HappeNiN' to me? What's HAPPENIN' to me¿ What's happenin' to me? What's happenin' to me? What's happenin' to me? What's 'nineppah   to me? What's happenin' to me? What's happenin' to me? What's happenin' to me? What's happenin' to me? What's happenin' to me? What's happenin' to me? What's happenin' to me? What's happenin' to me? **What's** happenin' to me? What's happenin' to me? What's happenin' to me? What's happenin' to me? What's happenin' to me? **What's happenin' to me!** What'S HAPPENIN' to me? WHAT's hapP ENIN' to ME? What'S HAPP-E-NIN' TO ME? WHAT'S HAPPENIN' TO ME? What's happenin' to me? What's happenin' to me? What's happenin' to ME? WHAT's happenin' to m-e? What's HappeNiN' to me? What's HAPPENIN' to me? What's happenin' to **me**? What's happenin' to me? What's happenin' to me? What's happenin' to me? What's happenin' to me? What's happenin' to me? **TAHW SI HAPPENIN' OT EM!** What's happenin' to me? What's happenin' to me? What is happenin' to me? What is happenin' to me? What's happenin' to me? What's happenin' to me? **WHAT is happenin' to me!** What is happenin' to me? What is happenin' to me? What is happenin' to me? What is happenin' to me? **What is happenin' to ME!** What IS HAPPENIN' to me? WHAT's hapP ENIN' to ME? What IS HAPP-E-NIN' TO ME? WHAT IS HAPPENIN' TO ME? What is happenin' to me? What's happenin' to me? What's happenin' to ME? WHAT's happenin' to m-e? What's HappeNiN' to me? What's HAPPENIN' to me? **TAHW IS** happenin' to me? What is happenin' to me? What is happenin' to me? What's happenin' to me? What's happenin' to me? What's happenin' to me? What's happenin' to me? What's happenin' TO ME? What's happenin' to me? What is happenin' to me? What is happenin' to me? What's happenin' to me? What's happenin' to me? What is happenin' to me? What is happenin' to me? What's happenin' to me? What's happenin' to me? What is **'NINEPPAH'** to me¿ What's happenin' to me? What's happenin' to me? What's happenin' to me? What is happenin' to me? What is happenin' to me? **WHAT's happenin' to me!** What's happenin' to me? What's happenin' to me? What is happenin' to me? **What 's happenin' to ME!** What'S HAPPENIN' to me? WHAT is hapP ENIN' to ME? What IS HAPP-E-NIN' OT ME? WHAT IS HAPPENIN' TO ME? What is happenin' to me? What is happenin' to me? What is happenin' to ME? WHAT is happenin' to m-e? What is HappeNiN' to me? What is HAPPENIN' to me? **THAW si** happenin' to me? What is happenin' to me? What is **happenin'** to me? What is happenin' to me? What **is** happenin' to me? What is happenin' to me? What is happenin' to me? What is happenin' to me? What **is** happenin' to me? What is happenin' to me? What is **happenin'** to me? What is happenin' to me? tahW **is** happenin' to me? What's **happenin'** to me? What's happenin' **OT ME?** What   is   happenin'   to   me?   What's happenin'   to   me?   What's   is happenin'   to me?   What is   happenin'   to me?   **WHAT   IS   HAPPENIN'   TO   ME!**   tahw   si 'nineppah   ot   em?   What   is   h a p p e n i n' to   me?   What's   happenin'   to   me?   W h a t ' s h a p p e n i n' t o m e?   What 's   happenin' to   me?   What's   happenin'   to me? **What**'s **happenin'** TO ME?   HAPPENIN'   **'NINEPPAH   ?**   tahw
W   h   a   t ?¿

Slice
       For Anarcha

The assistants lay me on a wooden table
Scrubbed raw
    I breathe
They hold my head down
    I breathe
They smother my wrists
Panic sponges air from my lungs
But I breathe
They grab my knees
    I whisper *breathe*
Their knuckles turn
        White
            White
                White
As they shove my legs wide open
    I tell myself *please breathe*

What is happening to me?
To me?
Me?
Anxiety gags my voice
Words grip my tongue
Refusing to fly with the twister

Slice

The surgeon cuts into my vagina
I bleed
He rummages around my bladder
I bleed
He refuses me willow bark for my misery
I bleed

Slice

Humiliation rakes my body
My back arches
My wails wet the room
An apprentice collapses
The room shudders

The surgeon clothed in a crisp cotton white shirt
With rolled up sleeves
Does not ask me if I want the experiment
To stop
                Stop
                          Stop
                                  Slice

Does the surgeon see me?
     See
          Me
Does he notice
My drenched skin?
Fear bores into my arteries
My sobs cling to walls
Spit blisters my mouth
My lungs gasp

     I faint

While shock sedates my stress
My body
Spurns giving my life
To those who cannot create
The air I breathe

As the surgeon and his apprentices
Beat the walls with words
Only they understand

     I awake

When prodded
I shake
With each incision
Tears wither my flesh
My eyes say stop
Please stop
I beg you
Stop

The surgeon
Fixes his eyes
On the part of my body
I cannot see

But I feel

Me

Butterflies rise beneath my skin
I breathe

Still

I

Breathe

        Breathe

                Breathe

                        Slice

Blood Alive When Dead

Blood
Lie cold
On floor
Where dirt settle
Beneath my dead womb.

De blood
In my body
Still
Warm.

De blood
In my baby
Still
Warm.

My eyes see fog.

Ef I
Cain't see
Fo' me an' my baby

Who will?

Contraction Abuse Blues

Somedays contraction come
Aftah baby born
But dem ain't natural
No Lawd
Dem ain't natural
No Lawd

Dem come when Mastah Man kick me
Dem come when Missus punch me
Dem come when surgeon knife rip me
Dem come when Mastah Man an' Missus
Plough my womb an' babies into field

Dey bed crop
Wid fresh an' rottin' compost
Ov slave auction block shavin'
Scattered wid de bones ov our people

Cotton Legacy

When I look at de room,
I don' see nothin.'
Everythin' a mist.
Lak I'm meanderin' thro' farm scarred
Wid rotten cotton blooms.

Doctor Man slash
My brown bruised waist
As ef it a wounded apple,
Rip by birds
Dat peck away
Fo' deir own satisfaction.

I born wid skin
Sof' as a Moses-in-a-basket flowah
An' silky as lamb's-ears leaves,
But my head bang
Lak a broken glass window frame
Loose from it hinge.
When weatha wheeze an' whistle an' whine,
De window in my mind bash wid no rhythm.
Each crack pane
Let cobweb stuff up
My thought.

I hear Doctor Man voices.
Dem sound lak a bunch ov crow
Squawkin' an' yappin' 'bout me.
Dem stir empty words into dead air.

I thirsty.
My mouth feel lak it full ov bush moss an' muslin mesh.
My lips stick to one anotha.
My mouth tuck words behin' my throat.
My womb try talk to me.
She speak Mama-truelove.
I try hear her touch.
I wa'n't cuddle my arm
But I cain't move.
I miss myse'f
When I cain't caress myse'f.

I ask my body,
You in me
Even when you not wid me?

My body say yes,
My body say yes,
My body say yes.

Aftah De Surgery: What Happened To Me?

What happened to me? What HapPenEd to me? WHAT happened to ME? tahw deneppah ot em? WhaT hAppEned to me? What HAPPENED to me? What happened TO ME? What happened to me? WHAT happened to me? WHAT HAPPENED TO ME? WhaT hAppEned to me? What happened to me? What happened to me? What   happened   to   me? What happened to me? What happened to me? What happened to me? What happened to me? What happened to me? What happened to me? tahw deneppah ot em? What happened to me? What happened to me? What happened to me? What happened to me? What happened to me? What happened to me? What happened to me? What happened to me? What happened to me? What happened to me? What happened to me? What happened to me? What happened to me? What happened to me? What happened to me? What happened to me? What happened to me? What deneppah
to me? What happened to me? What happened to me? What happened to me?
                What happened to me? What happened to me?
What happened to me? What   DENEPPAH   to me ¿
What happened to me? What happened to me? What happened to me? What happened to me? What happened to me? What happened to me? What happened to me? What happened to me? What happened to me? What happened to me? What happened to me? What happened to me? What happened to me? **What happened to me? tahW happened ot me?** What happened to em? What happened to me? What **happened to me? What happened to me? What** happened to me? What happened to me? What happened to me? **What happened to me? What happened to me?** What happened to me? What happened to me? What **happened** to me? tahw deneppah ot em? **What happened to me? What happened to me¿**   What happened to me? What **happened**
to me? What **happened** to me? What happened to me? What happened to me? What happened to me? What **happened** to me? What **happened** to me? What happened to me? What happened to me? What **happened** to me? What **happened** to me? What **happened** to me? What happened to me? What **happened** to me? What **happened** to me? What happened to me? What happened to me? TAHw deneppah ot em? What happened to me¿ What happened to me? What happened to me? What happened to me? What happened to me? What happened to me? What happened to me? What happened to me? What **happened to me? What** happened to me? What happened to me? What happened to me? What happened **to me? What happened** to me? What happened to me? What happened to me? What happened to me? **What happened to me? What happened to** me! What happened to me? What happened to me? What **happened to me? What** happened to me? What happened to me? What happened to me? What happened **to me? What happened** to me? What happened to me? What happened to me? What happened to me? What happened to me? What happened to me? What happened to me? What happened to me? tahw deneppah ot em? What happened to me? What happened to me? What happened to me? What happened to me? What happened to me? **What happened** to me? What happened to me? What happened to me? TahW happened to me? tahW happened to me? What happened ot me? What happened to me? What happened to me? What happened to me? What happened to me? What happened to me? What happened to me? What happened to me?   What deneppah
 to me? **tahw deneppah ot em?**
What happened to me?   What happened to me? What happened to me? What happened to me?
What happened to me? What happened to me? What HapPenEd to me? WHAT happened to ME? WhaT hAppEned to me¿ What HAPPENED to me? What happened TO ME? What happened to me? WHAT happened to me? WHAT HAPPENED TO ME? WhaT hAppEned to me? **What** happened to me? What happened to me? tahw deneppah ot em? What happened to me? What happened to me? What happened to me? What happened to me? What happened to me? **What? Happened? DENEPPAH To? Me? ¿**

54

Trauma Shadows

Shadow hound me
Dem lak smoke dat don' nevah drift away
Dem fill my eyes
Till I cain't mek sense what's in front ov me
Dem smell lak rotten fruit mix wid vomit-sick
Sometime I get so use to de stink I don' notice it
But I always notice dat de shadow
Don' wear de mask dat grin an' lie
Cuz dem don' have to

De shadow change shape when dem feel lak it
Dem lean sideways
An' hunch dem back an' chase an' growl at me
Dem wa'n't me to run away from myse'f

Sometime dem bully my nightmare
Dem say I'm no-no-good
Dem say I'm not wort' nothin'
Dem say I'm trash
Dem say I ugly
Dem say I lie
Cuz I know no bettah
Dem say anythin' I say don' mean shit
Dem say what happen to me nevah happen

But how can somethin' dat nevah happen still happen?

Dem scurry into my vision—a raccoon scavengin' fo' dinnah
Dem try chain down
My wonderin' dreams
Dat see beyond what I see

Dem wa'n't me to believe
What I don' wa'n't to live

Sometime dem try to stand in front of me
So I don' see myse'f

Dem don' wa'n't me to see myse'f
No mo'

Dem wa'n't me to see dem face
As my own

Shadow

"Den Dis Baby Be Sleep"[4]

I lay my baby's droopy head
On my shouldah,
Pat his back again an' again,
"Den dis baby be sleep."

I rock my chile
To an' fro,
To an' fro.
I hum a hum Mama use' to hum,
"Den dis baby be sleep."

My lil' baby head nod
As he lean into my ches.'
He jerk up
Den fall asleep.
He jerk up
Den fall asleep.
My hand skim his hair
As ef I'm movin' my fingahs
Ovah de tops ov new grass.

I cushion my chile wid my arms,
Blow all ovah his face
So he cool down,
"Den dis baby be sleep."

---

[4] McGill, Alice, editor. *In the Hollow of Your Hand: Slave Lullabies*. Houghton Mifflin, 2000. Inspired by the lullaby, "Dese Lil' Toes," created by one or more Black innovators enslaved during the antebellum era.

Butterflies Breaking Through Chrysalises

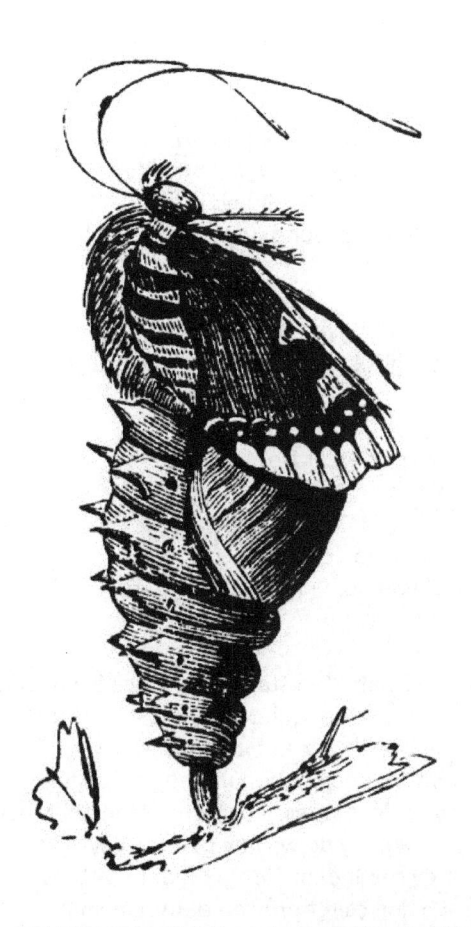

BUTTERFLY EMERGING
FROM ITS CHRYSALIS.

A Butterfly cain't break thro' a chrysalis widout a struggle.

Nanny Mama Parables—Survival

I
Silence talk to de heart
When de mouth cain't speak.

II
No shame in bein' afraid.

III
Don' build no bridge
Where land fall off land.
Don' build no bridge
Where ground don' feel yo' walk.

IV
Beware,
Straight talk don' always talk straight.

V
No one wear freedom de same way.

VI
You cain't rescue yo'se'f
Ef you don' know you need rescuin.'

VII
When Mastah Man stamp him voice in yo' skin,
Don' quiet yo' words.
Talk back to him in yo' spirit.
Live yo' imagination undah yo' tongue.
Throw yo' silent words at Mastha Man an' Missus.
Follow de way ov de runaway.
Dey rub Indian Turnip on dem clothes
So dog cain't prey on dem skin-smell
An' patrollah cain't shoehorn dem back into slavery.
Follow de way ov de runaway.
Let yo' rebellion out-sniff those dat try to sniff-you-out.
Mask yo' invisible insult an' uprisin,'
So Mastha Man an' Missus don' snare you.
An' let yo' sad-angry tears
Flood, flood, flood yo' heart
So it keep boomin' an' swellin' an givin.'

Blood Mothahs

Aftah my birth labor
Bring my beautiful baby into de world,
My body don' run right.
My mess
Crowd my pants,
Drip down my legs,
Wet my skirt.
De stink stick to me,
Feel lak pee burn my nostril.

Mama June Spring
Wash me till I smell lak tulip.
Mama May Wintah
Wipe me down
Wid kindness.
Mama April Sunlight
Scrub my clothes,
Soak dem in rivah watah.
Mama Mary Stream
Dress me in fresh skirt an' shirt
Every day.

Mama Margaret Goldie
Clean me
Wid rain watah,
Covah my body
Wid myrtle an' mountain mint.

When I stop feelin' pretty,
Mama Annette Honey
Braid peach coneflower into my cornrows.

When vein twitch in my head,
Mama Madeline rub lemon balm
On my forehead an' undah my nose.
She say lemon balm hunt out headache,
Relax muscle when it snarl-up
Lak a twisted dishrag.

Mama Bea say
When yo' tummy won't eat,
Parsley help you hungry fo' food.
When yo' recollection
Squirrel undergroun,'
Rosemary spark yo' memory

An' when upset needle me,
Mama Miss Ann
Rear roots
Dat nevah rot
So my skin
Feel love

Again.

Stillborn Wisdom Blues

        I

When baby dead weep.

When baby dead speak.

When baby dead sing.

When baby dead groan.

When baby dead sigh.

When baby dead scream.

When baby dead shout.

When baby dead hum.

When baby dead ramble.

When baby dead live.

        II

When baby dead,
Don' lose yo'se'f to death.

Grief de garden
You mus' watah.

Don' let grief die
Ef it won't die.

Don' put smile on grief face
Ef it don' laugh.

Love don' stand still
When baby still.

When yo' womb dead,
Love it wid life.

The Dawn Of A Sky

As dawn flays night
A lake stained by mist
Thaws in the sun
Haze threaded with droplets
Wanders into a tepid draught
Weaving across grounds
Shaggy with wild ginger

The sky looks
At her reflection
In the man-made lake
And fails to recognize herself

For so long
She had learned to see herself
Through the vision
Of this lake
Impaired by smog
Shrouded by dank borders

For so long
She had permitted
This lake
To be her eyes
To be her sky

She had forgotten
How to enfold
The fullness
Of her being

The sky
Muggy with the blues
Wonders if her reflection
In a clouded man-made lake
Can flood her distress

Does she need its blindness to see herself?

When Loss Astonishes

Air vexes my lungs.

Pounded by grief,
My body droops.

My limbs wilt
At the thought of stepping
Into another awareness.
On occasion I crave the impossible;
I imagine slipping into my dress pocket
And lying down amongst its lint lining.

My lungs gulp air.

Dread suckles on the prospect
That doom will breed further tragedies.
Paralysis cowers behind the ability
Of memories to recall stories
Insisting to be unforgotten.

My lungs exhale soundless air.

Weathered by mucus,
Saliva waxes the inside of my mouth.
Like the glue of summer haze,
The sodden remorse of silence
Cakes my loss with lament.

My lungs plead for air.

To speak means to relive
An existence dead to me,
While an open wound
Lanced with indifference
Resurrects limp sunflowers.
Though feeble, their brazen gold
Refuses to fade
In my mind.

How strange.
How astonishing.

Only then does blood arise,
Laid bare by dew
Flushed with saffron
Tomorrow.

When A Black Enslaved Nature Woman Philosophizes

Does night swallow constellations?
Does common milkweed cover her own scent with indigo?
Can day outlive dusk or survive without evening?

Hmmm

Can rain drown the sky?
Can steel-blue squalls chap the sun?
Can the earth rotate on her own whim?

Hmmm

Why can't a mirror reflect shadows?
Why can the moon shed shadows at night?
Can a shadow cloak another shadow?

Hmmm

Can a valley unchain herself
From barbwire weeds
Sprouting from soil
Where spicebush flourishes
With no end?

Hmmm

Watched[5]

I hold yo' cries
In my mouth.
Ef dem hear you upset
Dem will look fo' you.

"Mama's marster gwine sell us tomorrow,
Yes, yes—
Mama's marster gwine sell us tomorrow,
Yes, my child, watch and pray."

Ef dem see you giggle,
Blow bubbles
Wid yo' dribble.
Dem will steal you away from me.

"Mama's marster gwine sell us to 'Bama,
Yes, yes—
Mama's marster gwine sell us to 'Bama,
Yes, my child, watch and pray."

When dem grab you,
Dem will yank yo' head back,
Press dem thumb
Against yo' teeth,
Jam dem fingah
Aross yo' throat,
Clasp yo' legs,
Grip yo' arms,
Knead yo' scalp,
Pinch yo' fingahnail,
Crush yo' flat chest,
Punch yo' bottom,
Clutch yo' crotch,
Slap yo' hands,
Set a price,
Brand you,
Sell you
Wid a sneer.

"Yes, my child, watch and pray."

---

[5] McGill, Alice, editor. *In the Hollow of Your Hand: Slave Lullabies.* Houghton Mifflin, 2000. Inspired by the lullaby, "Watch and Pray," created by one or more Black innovators enslaved during the antebellum era.

Butterfly Movements

Butterflies don' fly in de same path in de same way at de same time.

Nanny Mama Parables—Wisdom

I
Kindness not always kind.

II
Wisdom yo' backbone.
Don' believe de lie dat what happen to you
Didn't happen.

III
Yo' heart de eye to yo' soul.

IV
De world cain't be chained.
Don' bind yo'se'f to chains
You nevah create.
Don' bind yo'se'f to chains
You create fo' yo'se'f.

V
Underground railroads don' build demse'f.
Some dream travel route where dream dead.
Don' numb yo' desire till it cain't believe no mo.'

VI
De eye cain't see what's goin' on behin' me
But wisdom let me see what I cain't see in front ov me.
We cain't be unseen
Ef we see ourse'f.

VII
Trouble cain't mek wisdom deaf
Cuz wisdom de ear widin de ear.
It hear sound dat no one hear.
It understan' what cain't be understood
By everyone, everythin.'
Storm cain't blind wisdom
Cuz wisdom de eye widin de eye.
It see thro' close eyelids
An' picture
What de eye cain't dream.

Secrets

LASH

Doctor Man tell me don' share
Him secrets wid no one

LASH

But he steal dese secrets
From me

LASH

Him talk lies
Play lak my idea him idea

LASH

He try beat silence
Into my skin

LASH

But quiet don' iron my mouth

LASH

My people
Keep on passin' on our secrets
Our herbal wisdom
Our workin' cure

LASH

Chillun

Don' let no Mastah Man or Missus
Shut up yo' tongue
Don' let no Mastah Man or Missus
Shut up we tongue
Don' let no Mastah Man or Missus
Shut up us tongue

LASH

Nanny Mama Medicine[6]

Drink gingah root tea
When stomach stamp her foot
Fevah cramp yo' muscle
Month blood thick
An' sting you lak nettle

When skin ragged
Mix spice bush wid sassafras
An' cornshuck wid watah
Den smooth spread it
On yo' body dat need soothin'

When nose drip
An' chill-thump
Drink Baume tea
Or Bayleaf tea
Or Hibiscus tea
Or Hackberry tree tea

When yo' belly
Wa'n't sweet anythin'
Burdock root
Will calm yo' cravin'

When belly affliction split you
Blackberry root tea
Will sew you back togetha

Boil jack-in-de-pulpit
When ulcer sniffle

Mix peppermint wid gingah an' honey
When belly throw food
Out yo' mouth

When flesh sick an' itch
Treat wid sasparilla

When skin break
An' yo' bones
Feel as ef ants bite dem
Up an' down
Treat wid blue curls

When head rattle
As ef rock hit rock
When cough cough rough
Put some stinkin' gum in a pouch
Wear it lak a necklace
To smell all day

When tooth ache
Chew blackberry leaves

Iron leaf
Stop yo' pee from peein'
All day

Sage cleanse room
Wid wisdom

An' don' forget:

Pass it on.
                      Pass it on.

                                          Pass it on . . .[7]

---

[6] For examples of herbs and remedies used by those of African descent enslaved during the antebellum era, see Herbert C. Covey, *African American Slave Medicine: Herbal and Non-Herbal Treatments*. Lexington Books, 2007.

[7] See Deirdre Cooper Owens, *Medical Bondage: Race, Gender, and the Origins of American Gynecology*. The University of Georgia Press, 2017, 51, 78, 80-82.

De Womb Tree

Befo' Doctor Man try steal
My womb
Befo' he poke it
Fix it beneath glass
Soak him medical paper
In my womb blood
Mama June Spring
Wisdom Mamas an' Papas
Ol' folk
Blood Mamas
De chillun
An' those on de othaside tek my womb
An' bury it
Next to de roots ov a pear tree
Where otha womb build deir home

Return

You cain't be created by anyone
Ef dey cain't create a comet.
So when Mastah Man an' Missus
Say you mus' drink bayou watah
An' tell you
Stop in yo' place,
Don' pay dem no mind.

Return to sky.
Tramp railroad track.
Pack earth from de ol' Mama country
Undah yo' nail.
Sow handprint in dirt.
Let mud dye yo' palm as if it charred yam.
Cup yo' nose wid both hand,
Inhale,
An' witness yo' spirit soar
Back to us.

Breathin' Don' Regret Breathin'

Baby girl,
Nevah regret de air you breathe,
Oh yes.

Don' breathe
Fo' Mastah Man an' Missus an' dem chillun,
Oh yes.

Don' let dem steal
Yo' breath fo' demse'f,
Oh yes.

Baby girl,
Hear me well:

Nevah say sorry fo' breathin'
Cuz breathin' don' ask nobody to breathe.

Yo' breath
Will nevah regret
Breathin' wid you.

Pause wid me well,
My baby girl.
Yo' breath
Live fo' you.

Pass It Forward

When you find a way to freedom,
Pass it forward.

When your words chop lynch ropes from trees,
Pass it forward.

When your laughter sings in your lungs,
Pass it forward.

When your lullabies huddle anxiety to sleep,
Pass it forward.

When your tears run without regret,
Pass it forward.

When you clamp rage sweaty in your fists,
Pass it forward.

When you speak gentle to your heart,
Pass it forward.

When you let bewilderment talk,
Pass it forward.

When you kneel for no one,
Pass it forward.

When you give birth to you,
Pass it forward.

Questions From a Son to a Mother

Can stairs be climbed if they don't exist?
      Can stairs be erected by me rather than *for me*?
           Can I decide where my stairs begin and land?

         Can I build my own stairs and climb them?
         Can we
           Scrub the wood
              And sand it down,
                  Even as nails and tacks
                        Resist being wrenched out?

Mama, when you say,
    "Baby-boy-son,
        Life ain't no crystal stair,
          But remember,
            Corners unfold hankerings
              Yet to be lived
                  In the what-ifs of our tomorrows,"
              Is that true?

        Mama, let's leave the crystal stair behind.
          It was never created for us.
            Isn't that true?

        Let us build new stairs together
          That take us where we want to go.
            Mama, will you climb these stairs

                              with me?

Yesterday Becoming

I lived with yesterday.
Built myself into yesterday.
Married my aspirations to yesterday.
Strapped my body into yesterday.
Turned yesterday into my home.
My prison.
My tomb.

Whenever yesterday called,
I answered.
Whenever she told me to smile,
I submitted.
Whenever she ordered me to go,
I followed.

Then one day,
I looked at yesterday.
I mean really stared at her.
I noticed her fatigue sagged
Like tree sap frozen by sun.
Fine gray hairs speckled her wrinkles.
Her sullen stare frowned away hope.
Her image
Trapped
In mirrors of histories
Fractured by unkempt promises,
Splintered into lives
Yet to be lived.

In that moment,
I realized
Yesterday had grown tired
Of being my today.

So, I decided to live into my new name:
Today, I will love tomorrow
And I will learn from the fires of yesterday
For this time and the next to come.

Grief Songs

When we swelter
In grief liturgies,
My tears sand away
The fear of feeling anything.

I wrap my arms
Across my chest
And rock.
I pat my arms
Up and down.
Down and up.

Sorrow moans
Mash up my words
Into mute rants.
Mutterings
Scale my stomach.
They burst
With each breath
Like steam spiraling
From a boiling pan.

My shoulders slouch.
I tilt my head back
Until my tears leave
Silver dust
On my cheeks.

This is what it means
To feel
Me.

Liberation

I

Your voice escapes.
You pursue her,
Catch up to her,
Walk with her,
Nuzzle into her wisdom.
You just need
To be close
Because she strengthens
You
To speak
For yourself.

She refuses
To be cuffed
By those determined
To hammer her words
Into silence.

So, your voice runs.
She scurries across swamplands,
Performs her own blues songs,
Exhales poems into life,
Digs underground railroads,
Bridges spirit-stories between wisdom-waterways.

Flanked by cotton fields,
Your voice,
Ingrained in the soil,
Declares:

Just as the moon
Cannot be removed
From the sky,
I will tend to my words of liberty
Growing in the garden of my mouth

II

At last,
I hear my voice.
She composes ballads
While my skin absorbs
A sublime love supreme.

No longer a bystander
To my own baptism,
My fingers lace between lyrics
I birthed into being.

We emerge as a refrain—
Sung
But not strained through a chorus,
Hummed
But not hemmed in,
Harmonized
But not immortalized.

Colored with ruby melodies,
Our timbres plume.

A riot of raucous audaciousness
Unrestrained by embarrassment
Infuses beauty into our rebellion.

Our music meditates on the lives
We have yet to assume
In our aspirations.

Suffused with sage-kissed honeysuckle,
We create the terrain we tread.
Our song stories
Disrobe dandelion feathers
Barren of shame.

Our verses watch berries ripen,
Let leaves fall in their own time
While our lyrics lift the earth skywards
As larks sing.

My Tongue

My tongue sits still
Until it feels safe enough
To moisten my mouth with words.

My tongue
Preserves griot folk songs
In her sheath.
She writes poetry
On the roof of my mouth.

Sometimes
My tongue plays dead.
She speaks in my thoughts.
She waits for me
To tell her when it is safe
To speak for myself,
For us.

Air Love

Jus' as de air won't sell you
Or stop bein' herse'f
So my love fo' you

—My sweet honey girl chillun
Delia an' Elizabeth
My sweet honey boy chillun
Washington an' William an' Oliver
My sweet honey chillun I didn't get to name or hold
An' my sweet honey chillun dat die befo' dem live—

My love fo' you
Wa'n't you to stay
Bein' yo'se'f

Jus' as de air don' choose
Who can tek her in dem lung
So my love fo' you
Sweet honey girl chillun
Delia an' Elizabeth
Sweet honey boy chillun
Washington an' William an' Oliver
An' all my chillun
Move free

Jus' as de air don' decide
When you can play wid it
So my love fo' you
Sweet honey girl chillun
Delia an' Elizabeth
Sweet honey boy chillun
Washington an' William an' Oliver
An' all my chillun
Jump jump jump
Ovah shootin' stars

Ancestors

Memories germinate
When they enflame rituals
Embedded in embers,
Set alight by those
Clinging to their will to survive.

Memories smolder.
They stand as torches
For others to find their way.

Forebearers cutback thickets
Knotted with freedom stories.
They give directions
To destinations
Mapped by the testimonies of yesterday people.
Future generations stumble upon
Uncharted roadways.
They stride on stony tracks
And discover amidst lavender-dusted thorns
The refusal of a people
Unwilling to unsee themselves
Or surrender to death.

In communion
With our soul-folk,
We journey on paths
Gnarled by brambles.

We walk through clearings
Our forerunners crossed
Under skies
Glossed with teal and marmalade

We are the beginning
Still becoming . . .

Way Up Yonder[8]

My sweet baby Liddy,
When you feel all alone,
Cry, baby, cry
To those
"Way up yonder"
Who hol' you
In de hollow ov deir hand,
In de hollow ov God hand.

Hear me sweet baby Liddy,
"Ol' Marster gwine suck sorrow.
Liddy, lay low.
Ol' Marster gwine suck sorrow.
Liddy, lay low."

When you scared,
Call out to those
"Way up yonder"
An' beside you
Who embrace you
In de hollow ov deir hand,
In de hollow ov God hand.

Listen well, sweet baby Liddy,
"Ol' Marster gwine suck sorrow.
Liddy, lay low.
Ol' Marster gwine suck sorrow.
Liddy, lay low."

When fury fume widin you,
Give yo' hurricane
To ancestors
"Way up yonder"
Who hear you
In de hollow ov deir hand,
In de hollow ov God hand.

Listen good, sweet baby Liddy,
"Ol' Marster gwine suck sorrow.
Liddy, lay low.
Ol' Marster gwine suck sorrow.
Liddy, lay low."

Yes, my sweet baby Liddy,
"Oh and it won't be long."
Dry yo' eye. Dry yo' eye.
De Promised Land
Rooted widin you
An' way up yonder.

Today, sweet baby Liddy,
"Ol' Marster gwine suck sorrow."
Today, sweet baby Liddy,
"Ol' Marster gwine suck sorrow."
No need to lay low no mo,'
No need to crawl no mo,'
No need to shelter no mo'
In de hollow ov yo' hands.

Rise up Liddy,
Rise up!

De time is now.
De time is now.
De time is now.

---

[8] McGill, Alice, editor. *In the Hollow of Your Hand: Slave Lullabies*. Houghton Mifflin, 2000. Inspired by the lullaby, "Liddy Lay Low," created by one or more Black innovators enslaved during the antebellum era.

Full Circle Butterfly Unbroken By Life

SARPEDON.—*Papilio sarpedon.*   HECTOR.—*Papilio hector.*

Butterfly Still Here,
Deir Cycle Dem Own.

Nanny Mama Parables—Birth Cycle

I
Life give birth to you,
You give birth to life.
Be de giver an' receiver ov life.

II
We don' breathe by ourse'f.
Our ancestors breathe wid us,
God breathe in us,
We breathe fo' generations to come.

III
No one can mek us invisible.
No one can unborn us
Ef we remembah ourse'f.

IV
Love build a home in our bones.
A Mama ain't a Mama by herse'f,
She need de lovin' ov othahs.

V
No one person can break irons wid deir own hand.
Only a people wid God can do dat.

VI
We precious.
We sacred.
We not dead to God,
God not dead to us.
Jus' as trees nevah forget us,
A Mama's womb de tree ov de world.

VII
Dere'll be times
When we won't wa'n't to keep climbin'
Stairs dat seem to go nowhere.
Dese de stairs
Where light find no light.
Sometimes we'll fall.
Some ov us won't wa'n't to get back up
An' sometimes we won't.

When we strap sack
On our beaten-down back,
We'll wa'n't to stop climbin.'
Dat's alright,
Dat's alright.
We'll res' a while.
Fo' love
Don' sleep,
Don' sleep.

VIII

Don' shame courage fo' hidin.'
Find it, hug it, rock it,
An' when it ready,
Walk wid it into open field
An' let it become.
Hear what I say,
Sometime de courage ov othas can be our own.
Listen wid yo' ears,
Sometime courage need company.

IX

Life an' death hol' hands.
Dem cousins,
Fragile as eggshell.
Death an' life bear fruit.
Death not dead to life.
Life not dead to death.

X

Don' ask fear
To be free ov fear.
Only love can release fear.
Chillun born new to dis earth
An' de earth new to dem.
Don' let yo' chile live in ol' skin.

XI

We mo' dan one beginnin.'

XII

We won't let our memories turn to dust.
We won't change our stories into an imagination.

We will say what has been said,
We will say what has been unsaid.
We will unsay de sayins' meant to kill us,
We will say what we wa'n't to say.
We won't undream our dreams fo' nobody.

Wisdom ain't no back door.
De back ov de line ain't our birth home,
Our kin,
Our friend.
We pass
De back an' middle an' front ov de line.

We won't mek suff'rin our only song.
We won't mek suff'rin our only story.
We won't mek suff'rin our only past.

Our labor pain nurse poetry.
Poetry our breas' milk.
Poetry speak our mind.
Poetry our name.
Our name.
Our name.

Sometime life lak labor trouble.
You don' know when
De pressure will come an' go,
It can strike you dizzy.
You hope terror wounds
Won't stay open, always.
You grasp de truth
Dat love don' colonize de air,
Beauty don' end,
Blood nevah drown,
Fresh breeze nevah grow stale.

A Poetic Memorial for Black Mothers—Past and Present and the Future

I met Anarcha by accident. I was not looking for her. She found me. While conducting research on the psychological and physiological symptoms of racial trauma, I came across an August 2017 news story documenting a protest organized by the activist group, Black Youth Project 100. In a photo capturing this moment, several young Black female adults stood in front of an 1890 statue of the nineteenth-century surgeon, J. Marion Sims, who was born in 1813 in South Carolina. The ironclad image of Sims positioned in a New York square was "installed across the street from the New York Academy of Medicine in 1934, with a plaque praising Sims' 'brilliant achievement.'"[9] For decades, many heralded Sims as the "father of modern gynecology"—a colonizing and Eurocentric moniker that erases the midwifery practices cultivated by Black women of the African diaspora.[10] The activists surrounding Sims' statue each wore a hospital gown daubed with red blotches around the abdomen and vagina. These blooms of blood-like stains symbolized the butchery countless Black enslaved mothers suffered when Sims and other medical practitioners operated on them after difficult labors. These women endured a condition called obstetric fistula, which occurs when "there is an opening between the vagina and also the bladder or the vagina and the rectum, which usually comes after traumatic childbirth."[11] This physical and psychological racial trauma left women unable to control their bladder and bowel movements.

Sims realized that the bourgeoning arena of women's medicine would enable him to amass wealth while elevating his professional standing. He started experimenting on Black enslaved women in the mid 1840s.[12] These women "became props in his journey of scientific discovery"[13] while he oversaw countless unsuccessful surgeries.[14] Despite these setbacks, Sims' deep seated insecurities fueled his unbridled ambitions. Medical historian and scholar Deirdre Cooper Owens stresses that "between 1844 and 1849, Sims experimented exclusively on enslaved women's bodies to aid him in locating the cure for this troublesome gynecological condition."[15] J. C. Hallman marks 1846 as the year in which Sims performed "a yearslong series of experimental vaginal surgeries . . . on approximately ten enslaved women." During this period, Sims conducted his "backyard operations"— also known as a "Negro Hospital"—primarily in Montgomery, Alabama.[16] Legal expert and professor Dorothy Roberts points out that Sims performed untried exploratory surgeries "on female slaves purchased expressly for his experiments."[17] She adds that doctors commonly carried out their investigative medical tests on these "women before practicing new surgical procedures on white women."[18] And yet, in their quest to establish their reputations, Sims and his numerous counterparts also performed invasive surgeries on poor Irish women.[19] Alternatively, white wealthy patrons desperate to cure their maladies paid significant sums to undergo untested surgical procedures.[20] Their treatments did not always lead to a satisfactory outcome. In several cases, the methods driving these gruesome surgeries cost women—whatever their status—their lives.[21] Anarcha was seventeen years old when Sims first experimented on her in his search to find a remedy for obstetric fistula. Over the course of five years, he operated on Anarcha thirty times without the aid of anesthesia.[22] While trying to perfect his surgical technique, Sims invited other physicians to observe his operations on Anarcha and other Black enslaved women such as Lucy and Betsey, whom he also mentions in his medical notes.

How did Anarcha, Lucy, and Betsey survive such traumatizing invasions of their bodies? What impact did these surgeries have on their physiological and psychological health? How did they mother their children as they tried to heal? Who cared for Anarcha, Lucy, and Betsey as distress overcame their bodies and spirits? What hopes did they have for their children when they carried their babies in their wombs? What role did community play in caring for these pregnant Black women who tried to cope with the infirmity of obstetric fistula?

Records show that "Anarcha was born on the Westcott plantation in Montgomery, Alabama. In 1833, she was seven years old, perhaps a year or two younger or older."[23] She died on June 27, 1869, after the abolition of slavery. She was buried in a cemetery in King George County, Virginia. The inscription on her headstone illuminates her lasting legacy. Her first name on her headstone is spelled Annacay, not Anarcha. This decolonization of her name can be upheld as an act of creolization. In this vein, Annacay and her people stamped their linguistic authority on dominant expressions of language by re-envisioning their names and articulating their own stories. Instead of associating her last name with her first enslavers, the Westcotts, Annacay shared her last name with her husband, Laurenzi Jackson. As a testament of their love, Annacay and Laurenzi—who in most primary materials is referred to as Lorenzo—are buried together. Their names herald a different identity unbound by stereotypes and half-truths. Abiding in this spirit of resistance, the remaining segment of this essay will refer to Anarcha as Annacay and Lorenzo as Laurenzi. Trawling through numerous primary materials, J. C. Hellman notes that though J. Marion Sims mentions Anarcha Westcott in his autobiography, Hellman found "no document to suggest that Anarcha took the name of her former enslaver."[24] This kind of discrepancy underscores Sims's suspect remedies, flawed 'discoveries,' and "fanciful narrative that brought him fame and fortune."[25] The unearthing of Sims' problematic surgical vices curdles his professional reputation and exposes his toxic legacy.

Certainly, Annacay endured unimaginable experiments of surgical butchery that were neither fanciful nor a fantasy. And yet, while enduring such violations of the human body, Annacay opened herself to receive and give love. As an herbalist and midwife, Annacay gained knowledge of the healing power of herbs and body wisdom through ancestral customs.[26] Annacay cared for many mothers—enslaved and enslavers—and their children.[27] She was a blood mother. Academic Deirdre Cooper Owens fleshes out the concept of the blood mother by explaining that "'[b]lood' served as a metaphor for West African mothers and their descendants who were born in America. It contained both good and bad essences and forged ties among black women that were both secret and sacred. Life and death were contained in the blood, from the release of menstrual blood and blood lost during miscarriages to the symbolic use of blood as a mode for purification."[28] This cosmological and philosophical life pulse coursed through Annacay's desire to give birth to several children. Despite living with a condition that made it difficult to control her bladder and bowel movements, Annacay shared her body, mind, and spirit with others. She believed she was touchable and loveable. She was willing to touch, love, and heal others in return. She nurtured community members through their ailments and concerns. Though some of her children were sold to enslavers, and though she suffered miscarriages, Annacay raised Delia, Washington, Elizabeth, William, and her husband's daughter, Louisa.[29] The words "Gone But Not Forgotten" stand at the base of the headstone she shares with her husband, who died 15 years after her passing on September 28, 1884. He never remarried.[30] In "a comprehensive catalog of all the known cemeteries in King George County, there was just one entry for the former Alto property: a single grave for Annacay and Laurenzi Jackson."[31] Hallman speculates that "the stone marking Anarcha's Virginia grave appears to have been placed long after she and Lorenzo died, which would account for why the spelling of their names and the dates of their deaths differ from earlier records. The stone itself is an ongoing mystery. Who created it, and how was such an ungainly monument transported to a hidden and quite rugged piece of land?"[32] Notwithstanding these mysteries, Annacay and Laurenzi's final headstone reminds us that "a butterfly don' love jus' anybody,"[33] because choosing love cannot be contained by slavery.

To comprehend and heal from trauma, survivors of systemic brutality must, in their time, acknowledge and confront what happened to them. Making sense of harrowing revelations can often be too hard to bear. At the same time, morbid fascination with parading Black bodies for public consumption can cause many to withdraw from understanding how racism has impacted them—a necessary component for healing. A preoccupation with the atrocities Black people confront frequently veils the white gaze. *Birthing Butterflies* refuses to feed or gorge on what Toni Morrison calls "the hunger for other people's pain."[34] Instead, it summons "the true folk blues poem" ethos that possesses a "range of implications, imagery, character, mood, wonder, or surprise."[35] This manuscript also embodies the "manner of the blues" by inviting "greater flexibility of imaginative and experiential territory."[36] Black English in its various forms permeates the poems in this book. The works and lives of Paul Laurence Dunbar, Harriet Tubman, Sojourner Truth, Fredrick Douglass, Countee Cullen, Langston Hughes, Zora Neale Hurston, Wallace Thurman, Toni Morrison, August Wilson, Ntozake Shange, Suzan-Lori Parks, Lynn Nottage, Pete Rock & C.L. Smooth, Queen Latifah, Lauryn Hill, Missy Elliot, Salt-N-Peppa, Tupac Shakur (2Pac), DMX, Kendrick Lamar, J. Cole, Scar Face, Snoop Dogg, Public Enemy, Bktherula, Megan Thee Stallion, Cardi B, Gil Scott-Heron and countless other Black creatives and activists illustrate that linguistic formulations of the African diaspora find expression in the US Black vernacular. Similarly, Black enslaved peoples spoke for themselves and confronted oppressive systems bent on treating them inhumanely. They did not wait for society to confirm their human worth. They recognized their capacity to embrace what the prolific poet and essayist June Jordan calls "the language of their Black lives."[37] For Jordan, Black English is neither "*non*-standard"[38] nor "*sub*-standard."[39] She insists that "Black language . . . is not A Mistake, or A Verbal Deficiency. It is a communication system subsuming dialect/regional variations that leave intact, nevertheless, a language that is invariable in profound aspects."[40] In keeping with Jordan's assertions, the poems in *Birthing Butterflies* conjure ancestral, poetic, vital, political, and intimate expressions of Black English.

Additionally, the religious traditions and collaborative agency observed in these poems channel the concept of the "invisible institution."[41] Black human beings enslaved within an oppressive society spearheaded supportive systems fostering self and communal care that were largely invisible to beneficiaries of a racialized and abusive economic system. Poetic renditions of history can illustrate how the body retains manifestations of trauma. To borrow the term coined by Bessel van der Kolk, the poetry in this work "keeps score" as it explores the physiological, psychological, and spiritual manifestations of trauma stomached by so many who confront what Toni Morrison calls "[t]he insanity of racism"[42]—a warped mindset fixated on normalizing racial social constructs as unharmful, even as racism makes many sick with its disease. The mythology that Black people can tolerate agony more than their white counterparts abounds. The implications of such dangerous and misinformed racialized views contribute to how Black mothers encounter medical racism well into the current century. According to an article published by the Centers for Disease Control and Prevention (CDC) on April 3, 2023, "Black women are three times more likely to die from a pregnancy-related cause than White women."[43] As the CDC notes, numerous dynamics influence these discrepancies, "such as variation in quality healthcare, underlying chronic conditions, structural racism, and implicit bias. Social determinants of health prevent many people from racial and ethnic minority groups from having fair opportunities for economic, physical, and emotional health."[44] The social factors impacting Black maternal mortality rates are even more devastating given that "more than 80% of pregnancy-related deaths in the U.S. are preventable."[45] The individuals in these poems have the freedom not to participate in what Regina King calls "emotional aerobics"[46] that feed into perceptions of how those who lived through slavery ought to conduct themselves. Their humanity is not preoccupied with disproving stereotypes or pacifying caricatures in order to justify their existence. Their stories denounce practitioners that medically abuse Black women's bodies in the name of science. By recognizing the histories of Black mothers, the opportunities to ponder their sacred lives are endless. For historical purposes, *Birthing Butterflies* acknowledges the herbal cures and practices observed by Black enslaved mothers and community members. It does not endorse any medication or therapy featured in this work as the means through which contemporary pregnancies should be met. At the same time, the women in *Birthing Butterflies* can inspire us to learn how to care for and accompany Black mothers within various communities of care.

Birthing Butterflies aligns nineteenth-century Black enslaved mothers with the metamorphosis of butterflies, a symbol of transformation and resurrection. Like a cocoon, their wombs nurture and give birth to memories that sustain Black life.

Just as butterflies take flight from the confines of their self-built shells, these poems mine how Black enslaved mothers experience Black love, joy, anguish, freedom, and rebirth. *Birthing Butterflies* offers a humane appreciation of the vital spirit and robust legacy of Black enslaved mothers. Amidst a violent socio-economic and predatory slave system, this collection of poems begins with Black love. Black enslaved people uphold each other's priceless and treasured dignity. They affirm James Baldwin's assertion that "a baby does not come into the world merely to be the instrument of someone else's profit."[47] Black enslaved mothers embody the vulnerability, fight, and emotional transparency of the blues. They invoke the agency of the spirituals and inhabit the depths of African diasporic cosmologies. Their wisdoms relish the linguistic ingenuity of Black English and revel in the dialectal flair of creole. Their creation of nursery rhymes and lullabies marry with the dissonant timbres of jazz and the exultations of lament. As memory keepers, their testimonies sing griot chronicles. In *Birthing Butterflies*, Black enslaved women become a sacred harbor as they abide in processes of luscious becoming for themselves and generations to come.

---

[9] Domonoske, Camila. "'Father Of Gynecology,' Who Experimented On Slaves, No Longer On Pedestal In NYC." NPR, 17 Apr. 2018, www.npr.org/sections/thetwo-way/2018/04/17/603163394/-father-of gynecology-who-experimented-on-slaves-no-longer-on-pedestal-in-nyc.

[10] See: Cooper Owens, Deirdre Benia. *Medical Bondage: Race, Gender, and the Origins of American Gynecology.* University of Georgia Press, 2021; Washington, Harriet A. *Medical Apartheid: The Dark History of Medical Experimentation on Black Americans from Colonial Times to the Present.* 1st Anchor books (Broadway Books) edition., Anchor Books, 2008; Giddings, Paula. *When and Where I Enter: The Impact of Black Women on Race and Sex in America.* 1st ed., W. Morrow, 1984; White, Deborah G. *Ar'n't I a Woman?: Female Slaves in the Plantation South.* Norton, 1985; Roberts, Dorothy. *Killing the Black Body, Race, Reproduction, and the Meaning of Liberty.* Vintage, 2014; www.pbs.org/newshour/show/alabama-artist-works-to-correct-historical-narrative-around-beginnings-of-gynecology

[11] "Remembering Anarcha, *Lucy, and Betsey: The Mothers of Modern Gynecology.*" NPR, 16 Feb. 2016, www.npr.org/transcripts/466942135.

[12] Hallman, J.C. Say Anarcha: *A Young Woman, a Devious Surgeon, and the Harrowing Birth of Modern Women's Health.* Macmillan., 2023, ix.

[13] "Remembering Anarcha, *Lucy, and Betsey: The Mothers of Modern Gynecology.*" NPR, 16 Feb. 2016, www.npr.org/transcripts/466942135.

[14] Ibid.

[15] Cooper Owens, Deirdre Benia. *Medical Bondage: Race, Gender, and the Origins of American Gynecology.* University of Georgia Press, 2021, 36.

[16] Hallman, J.C. Say Anarcha: *A Young Woman, a Devious Surgeon, and the Harrowing Birth of Modern Women's Health.* Macmillan., 2023, ix.

[17] Roberts, Dorothy. *Killing the Black Body, Race, Reproduction, and the Meaning of Liberty.* Vintage, 2014, 167.

[18] Ibid.

[19] Cooper Owens, Deirdre Benia. *Medical Bondage: Race, Gender, and the Origins of American Gynecology.* University of Georgia Press, 2021, 4-11.

[20] See: Hallman, J. C. *Say Anarcha: A Young Woman, a Devious Surgeon, and the Harrowing Birth of Modern Women's Health.* Macmillan, 2023.

[21] See: Hallman, J. C. *Say Anarcha: A Young Woman, a Devious Surgeon, and the Harrowing*

Birth of Modern Women's Health. Macmillan, 2023; Washington, Harriet A. *Medical Apartheid: The Dark History of Medical Experimentation on Black Americans from Colonial Times to the Present*. 1st Anchor books (Broadway Books) edition., Anchor Books, 2008.

[22] Cooper Owens, Deirdre Benia. *Medical Bondage: Race, Gender, and the Origins of American Gynecology*. University of Georgia Press, 2021, 38.

[23] Hallman, J. C. Say Anarcha: *A Young Woman, a Devious Surgeon, and the Harrowing Birth of Modern Women's Health*. Macmillan, 2023, 7.

[24] Ibid., xii.

[25] Ibid., xi.

[26] See: Hallman, J. C. *Say Anarcha: A Young Woman, a Devious Surgeon, and the Harrowing Birth of Modern Women's Health*. Macmillan, 2023.

[27] Ibid.

[28] Benia, Deirdre & Cooper Owens. *Medical Bondage: Race, Gender, and the Origins of American Gynecology*. University of Georgia Press, 2021, xlv-xlvi.

[29] See: Hallman, J. C. *Say Anarcha: A Young Woman, a Devious Surgeon, and the Harrowing Birth of Modern Women's Health*. Macmillan, 2023.

[30] Ibid., 368.

[31] Ibid., xiv-xv.

[32] Ibid., ii.

[33] May, C. *Birthing Butterflies*. Finishing Line Press, 2024, 1.

[34] Morrison, Toni. "Toni Morrison, The Art of Fiction No. 134." Interview by Elissa Schappell and Claudia Brodsky Lacour. *The Paris Review*, 28 Sept. 2020.

[35] Jones, Gayl. *Liberating Voices: Oral Tradition in African American Literature*. Penguin Books, 1992.

[36] Ibid., 27.

[37] Jordan, June. *Civil Wars*. First Touchstone edition, Simon & Schuster, 1995, 66.

[38] Ibid., 65.

[39] Ibid.

[40] Ibid., 67.

[41] Raboteau, Albert J., *Slave Religion: The "Invisible Institution" in the Antebellum South*. Oxford University Press, 2004.

[42] Interviewed by Elissa Schappell & Claudia Brodsky Lacour. "Toni Morrison, The Art of Fiction No. 134." *The Paris Review*, 28 Sept. 2020, www.theparisreview.org/interviews/1888/the-art-of-fiction-no-134-toni-morrison.

[43] "Working Together to Reduce Black Maternal Mortality." *Centers for Disease Control and Prevention*, 8 Apr. 2024, www.cdc.gov/healthequity/features/maternal-mortality/index.html.

[44] Ibid.

[45] Ibid. Also see: "Pregnancy-Related Deaths: Data from Maternal Mortality Review Committees in 36 US States, 2017–2019." Centers for Disease Control and Prevention, 19 Sept. 2022, https://www.cdc.gov/maternal-mortality/php/data-research/mmrc-2017-2019.html?CDC_AAref_Val=https://www.cdc.gov/reproductivehealth/maternal-mortality/erase-mm/data-mmrc.html; Stafford, Kat. "Why Do so Many Black Women Die in Pregnancy? One Reason: Doctors Don't Take Them Seriously." The Associated Press, 23 May 2023, https://projects.apnews.com/features/2023/from-birth-to-death/black-women-maternal-mortality-rate.html

[46] Rose, Steve. *The Guardian*, 8 Jan. 2021, www.theguardian.com/film/2021/jan/08/regina-king-one-night-miami-oscar-winning-beale-street-actor-black-lives-matter.

[47] Baldwin, James. "An Open Letter to My Sister, Miss Angela Davis." *The New York Review of Books*, 19 Nov. 1970, www.nybooks.com/articles/1971/01/07/an-open-letter-to-my-sister-miss-angela-davis/.

Acknowledgments

I am indebted to my parents who encouraged me to cultivate my dreams. As a family and community, we confronted systemic biases daily. I attended schools in a borough where very few teachers nurtured or believed in the academic potential of the young people living in the East End of London. But many still tried and succeeded to create meaningful lives.

I wish to thank my mentors, Dr. Margaret B. Wilkerson, Dr. Barbara T. Christian, June Jordan, and Dr. Margarita Melville for shaping my academic interests, nurturing my intellectual curiosity, and helping me develop my artistic craft in poetry, theater, and literary criticism.

I wish to thank Anthony Bankes, Suzi Nelson, and Kelly Elaine Navies for reading drafts of my work in its evolution stages.

I am deeply thankful to the following individuals for writing blurbs for *Birthing Butterflies*: Kao Kalia Yang, an author I have long admired and whose works are a staple in my required reading course list; Dr. Katherine Clay Bassard, an outstanding and groundbreaking scholar; Kelly Elaine Navies, a consummate oral historian and poet; and Julia Dinsmore, whose writings inspire me. Dinsmore coined a term that shaped a line in one of my poems, "Nanny Mama Parables—Wisdom." In this piece, I engage with Dinsmore's "eye in an eye" philosophy by folding this ethos of foresight and hindsight into the language of Black English and creole.

The poems featured in *Birthing Butterflies* initially stemmed from the research I conducted on the relationship between psychology, racial trauma, and poetic storytelling during my time as a Scholarship and Christianity in Oxford (SCIO) Visiting Scholar in Science and Religion. This SCIO initiative was "sponsored by a grant given by Bridging the Two Cultures of Science and the Humanities II, a project run by Scholarship and Christianity in Oxford, the UK subsidiary of the Council for Christian Colleges and Universities, with funding by Templeton Religion Trust and The Blankemeyer Foundation."

I wish to thank the publishers of *Families, Systems & Health* (37, [3], 270-272) for publishing an earlier version of my poem, "Slice."

I am grateful for the generous financial support of the Minnesota section of the American College of Obstetricians and Gynecologists (ACOG), the Worshams, and the Phenows for enabling me to distribute free copies of *Birthing Butterflies* to Black mothers.

Finally, I want to thank my grandparents, members of the Windrush Generation, whose sacrifices and love helped make me into the woman I am becoming today.

Notes - Illustrations in *Birthing Butterflies*

Front Cover Image	Front Cover	Unsplash-kK8zDf-Vqw
Image 1	ix	istockphoto-92337356
Image 2	x	istockphoto-455687245
Image 3	Page 1	istockphoto- 1423998094
Image 4	Page 2	istockphoto-455687245
Image 5	Page 14	istockphoto-488309378
Image 6	Page 15	istockphoto-455687245
Image 7	Page 29	istockphoto-910120368
Image 8	Page 30	istockphoto-455687245
Image 9	Page 41	istockphoto- 488654603
Image 10	Page 42	istockphoto-455687245
Image 11	Page 57	istockphoto- 910120078
Image 12	Page 58	istockphoto-455687245
Image 13	Page 66	istockphoto- 185123240
Image 14	Page 67	istockphoto-455687245
Image 15	Page 85	istockphoto-1689642940
Image 16	Page 88	istockphoto-455687245